pizzette

Little pizzas for appetizers, snacks, entrées, and more

By Lou Seibert Pappas

Illustrations by Robert Clyde Anderson

CHRONICLE BOOKS

SAN FRANCISCO

Acknowledgments

With many thanks to Judith Schwartz for testing recipes and to Stanford University professor Dina Viggiano for sharing her Italian expertise.

Library of Congress Cataloging-in-Publication Data:

Pappas, Lou Seibert.
　　　　Pizzette : little pizzas for appetizers, snacks, entrées, and more / by Lou Pappas ; illustrated by Robert Clyde Anderson
　　　　　　　p.　　cm.
　　　　Includes index.
　　　　ISBN 0-8118-1189-1
　　　　1. Pizza.　I. Title
TX770.P58P37 1996
641.8'24 — dc20　　　　　　　　　　　　　　　　　95-9504
　　　　　　　　　　　　　　　　　　　　　　　　　CIP

Book design by Martine Trélaün

Printed in Hong Kong.

Distributed in Canada by Raincoast Books,
8680 Cambie Street
Vancouver, B.C. V6P 6M9

10　9　8　7　6　5　4　3　2　1

Chronicle Books
275 Fifth Street
San Francisco, CA 94103

contents

Pizzette, or little pizzas, are wonderful individual treats. In sizes ranging from 4 to 6 inches, they are perfect for eating out of hand at any time of day.

Ideal for serving one or two people, pizzette make delectable appetizers, first courses, main dishes, and even desserts. Being able to sample two or more kinds at an occasion enhances their charm.

These tantalizing little pies inspire impromptu, worldly combinations of toppings and crusts. Flavors can vary widely, from conventional Italian toppings to inventive combinations using foods from other cuisines. The crusts may range from basic to such savory variations as whole-wheat bran, rosemary-sage, four-grain, buckwheat, and saffron, to sweet doughs for dessert pizzette.

Mixing pizzette dough takes just a few minutes and may be done in advance. It will keep refrigerated for two days for successive bakings on several occasions. Rolling out the rounds may seem slow until a rhythm is achieved, then they go swiftly.

The dough may be frozen in well-wrapped sections or it may be frozen in rounds. Let it thaw before baking. Prebaked untopped crusts may also be well wrapped and frozen. Let them thaw, top, and bake as directed. Some, but not all, sweet and savory pizzette can be frozen.

Though appetites vary widely, plan to serve two or three 4-inch pizzette per person for appetizers and two or three 6-inch pizzette for an entrée. Figure on two 4-inch sweet pizzette for dessert and two or three 6-inch sweet pizzette for a brunch entrée. One batch of dough makes two dozen 4-inch pizzette or sixteen 6-inch pizzette.

May you become enraptured with the fun of pizzetta making, turning out these free-form cartwheels to delight diners any time of day.

Pizza/Pizzas, Pizzetta/Pizzette

From ancient Egyptian tombs to the walls of Pompeii, painted scenes depict the history of round flat breads, the hearth breads baked on hot stones or clay discs that were the forerunners of pizza.

Pizza has been a beloved peasant staple for millennia. The street vendors of Naples sold the robust leavened bread to the poor, who had no ovens to bake their own. In America, the first pizzeria was opened by Gennaro Lombardi in New York City in 1905. But it was really the GIs returning from southern Italy after World War II who popularized this simple food that has spawned a multibillion-dollar industry.

Pizza is now popular worldwide. An abundance of pizzerias and a wide selection of frozen pies has made pizza easily available. Homemade pizza is in a category all its own, however: The freshest and most satisfying pie is the one you make yourself with exactly the topping or toppings you want.

In Italian, the word *pizza* becomes *pizze* in the plural. In the same way, *pizzetta* in Italian becomes *pizzette* in the plural. So assimilated has pizza become in America, however, that here the word is given the American plural to become *pizzas*.

Pizzette, easy and quick to make, simpler to eat and more elegant than a wedge from a large pizza, are a delight for both friends and family.

INGREDIENTS

Pizzetta starts with a simple dough of flour, water, yeast, honey or sugar, salt, and olive oil. Toppings can be minimal or abundant.

Olive oil

Olive oil lends crispness to pizzetta crust and enhances the interior, providing a tender crumb. Brushing olive oil on the pizzette rounds contributes to a golden brown color. Extra-virgin olive oil, the premium, or best, quality, is preferred for its rich, fruity flavor. Olive oils labeled "virgin" or "pure" are less fruity and lighter tasting. Butter lends a tenderness to the crust of sweet doughs. Canola oil may be used for greasing a pan if minimal flavor is desired.

Flour

Unbleached all-purpose flour, a blend of hard and soft wheats, makes an excellent crust. Bread flour has a high gluten content that raises yeast dough to its maximum volume, but the dough requires considerable working or kneading to make it respond properly. Unless you are willing to knead the dough thoroughly, sometimes 10 minutes or more, you will achieve a better product with unbleached flour. Semolina flour also contributes to a textured crust. Other flours, such as whole wheat, rye, cornmeal, barley, chestnut, and buckwheat, add another flavor dimension to pizza. Because they are heavier and contain less gluten, these flours should be used in small amounts in combination with unbleached all-purpose flour.

Cheeses

Though not essential, cheese lends an unctuous creaminess to pizzette as long as it is not overcooked. Fresh mozzarella, which is stored in water, melts into a malleable, smooth mass. Factory-made mozzarella is best shredded rather than sliced to avoid a rubbery mass. Combining two cheeses often results in a more interesting flavor. Good cheeses to blend with mozzarella include Gruyère, Jarlsberg, Monterey jack, Fontina, Muenster, and white Cheddar. The rinds of cheeses such as Brie or Camembert should be removed and discarded before the cheese is used. Triple-cream cheeses,

natural cream cheeses, goat cheeses, and mascarpone lend an elegant richness paired with fruits. The premium Parmesan cheese, Parmigiano Reggiano, lends a bright snappiness. By sprinkling it on after baking, the cheese remains moist and flavorsome. Other Parmesans or Asiago, pecorino romano, kasseri, or dry jack cheese can also lend a finishing touch. Low-fat cheeses tend to be rubbery when melted and should be omitted.

Vegetables

Choose peak-season, ultra-fresh vegetables for best flavor. The meaty Roma, or plum, tomatoes are a top choice when they are vine ripened. Oil-packed sun-dried tomatoes will remain moist during baking. Commercial sun-dried tomatoes can be bitter; choose carefully or make your own from in-season Roma tomatoes. Select mushrooms with tightly closed caps on the underside, so that the gills are hidden, for peak freshness. Yukon Gold potatoes have the advantage of retaining their golden color after baking.

Seafood and Meats

Cooked seafood such as shrimp, mussels, or smoked fish are best added to a topping after baking or during the last 2 minutes of baking to avoid toughening or drying them. Chicken breasts and ground meats should be precooked, as the baking time for pizzette is brief. Many specialty sausages are precooked and need only slicing and baking.

Herbs

Choose fresh herbs, such as basil, thyme, oregano, sage, parsley, rosemary, dill, cilantro, and tarragon. Often it is best to sprinkle them on after baking to avoid drying them out.

Pizzetta dough may be made by hand or by machine. A heavy-duty standing electric mixer mixes and kneads dough with ease. Because the amount of dough is small, a flat paddle attachment works well for both mixing and kneading. A food processor is satisfactory, but the dough will require extra kneading on a lightly floured board.

Baking Stone or Tiles

A baking stone or unglazed quarry tiles placed directly on the lowest oven rack provide an intense heat that radiates to make a crisp brown crust. While it is ideal to bake large pizzas directly on a stone or tiles, it is tedious for baking 6 to 8 pizzette at a time. Instead, place the pizzetta rounds on a pizza pan or baking sheet and place the pan directly on the preheated stone or tiles. You can also place a sheet of aluminum foil on a baker's paddle or a rimless baking sheet, arrange the pizzetta rounds on the foil, and slide the foil onto the stone or tiles. A small number of prebaked pizzette may be reheated directly on a stone or tiles; the direct heat will lend a marvelous crispness to the crusts. Preheat the oven to 425°F for 30 minutes with the stone or tiles on the lowest shelf of the oven, then bake the pizzette for 3 to 4 minutes, or until heated through.

Pans

Heavy baking sheets are ideal for baking pizzette, as are pizza pans or pizza screens, which are pizza pans with perforations. Since only one pan should bake in the center of the oven at a time, you will need 3 pizza pans or baking sheets to prepare an entire recipe at once, or you can use a sheet of aluminum foil if you have a baking stone or tiles (see the preceding paragraph). You may prefer to divide the pizzetta dough and bake it on successive days with different toppings.

Dough Scraper

A dough scraper with a wooden handle and a flexible metal blade is invaluable for cutting dough into small portions and for removing sticky dough from work surfaces.

Other Useful Tools

A pastry brush, a rolling pin, a heavy metal spatula, and a cutting board or serving tray are other useful items, besides such basics as mixing bowls and measuring utensils.

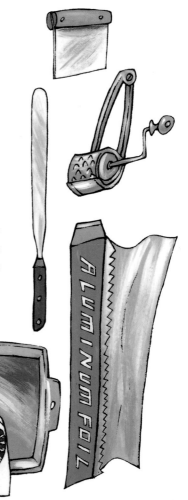

Because the moisture contents of flours may vary, slightly more or less flour than called for—from ¼ to ⅓ cup—may be needed to achieve a light, elastic consistency. Too much flour, added initially or kneaded in later, can make a heavy dough with a tough crust. Too little flour will make a sticky dough that is liable to tear during shaping. The ideal dough is springy, soft, and pliable.

The basic recipe specifies 2 teaspoons dry yeast, slightly less than a ¼-ounce (2½-teaspoon) package, because a slower rise with less yeast gives a more flavorful pizzetta. If you are in a hurry, you can use 1 package dry yeast instead.

Once the dough is mixed, place it in an oiled bowl, cover it with plastic wrap, and let it rise in a warm place, about 70° to 80°F, until doubled in size, about 1 to 1½ hours.

Once the dough has doubled, the pizzette can be shaped, assembled, and baked immediately. Or, you can punch the dough down and let it rise again before baking. This does not alter the crust, but it gives you more time if you need it before assembling and baking the pizzette. Or, you can refrigerate the dough for several hours or up to 2 days. It does not need to be punched down during this time. By letting the dough mature in the refrigerator, it becomes easier to handle and more elastic. Refrigerating also enhances the flavor of dough.

A dough scraper is useful for cutting the dough into sections. After each section of dough is flattened with your hand, use a floured rolling pin to roll it out to the desired size with just two or three rolls. Once all the balls of dough are rolled out and placed on the pan, the topping is sprinkled over them. Toppings that do not need much cooking, such as cooked shellfish, are added before the last 1 to 2 minutes of baking. Grated Parmesan cheese and fresh herbs are best sprinkled over pizzette after baking, to keep them from drying out.

Leftover pizzette may be refrigerated for 1 day and reheated. Bake them in a preheated 425°F oven, preferably directly on a preheated baking stone or tiles, until heated through, about 2 to 4 minutes.

Be selective when freezing already baked pizzette: Meats work best, and seafood, asparagus, golden squash, and broccoli should be avoided. Allow frozen pizza to thaw before reheating in a preheated 425°F oven for 3 to 4 minutes, or until crisp.

A basic dough can be varied with different flours, herbs, and other seasonings to achieve interesting flavors. Because cheese can dry out at high temperatures, it is is not used in the crust.

Basic Pizzetta Dough

2 teaspoons active dry yeast

1 cup warm water
(105° to 115°F)

1 teaspoon honey or sugar

2½ cups unbleached all-purpose flour

¾ teaspoon salt

2 tablespoons extra-virgin olive oil

Hand method

In a large bowl, sprinkle the yeast over the water and stir in the honey or sugar. Let stand until dissolved and foamy, about 10 minutes. Mix in 1 cup of the flour, the salt, and oil, stirring with a wooden spoon until smooth. Gradually add the remaining flour ½ cup at a time, beating until the dough pulls away from the sides of the bowl. Turn out on a lightly floured board and knead until smooth and elastic, about 5 minutes.

Heavy-duty electric mixer method

In a heavy-duty electric mixer bowl, sprinkle the yeast over the water and stir in the honey or sugar. Let stand until dissolved and foamy, about 10 minutes. Using the flat paddle attachment, mix in 1 cup of the flour, the salt, and oil. Gradually add the remaining flour ½ cup at a time and beat for 2 minutes, or until the dough clings together in a ball and is smooth and elastic. It is not necessary to knead by hand.

Food processor method

In a small bowl, sprinkle the yeast over the water and stir in the honey. Let stand until dissolved and foamy, about 10 minutes. Place the flour and salt in a food processor with the metal blade attached. Process for 5 seconds. Add the oil to the yeast mixture and, with the machine running, pour this mixture through the feed tube and process until the dough clings together in a ball, about 30 seconds. Turn out on a lightly floured surface and knead for 1 or 2 minutes.

Place the dough in an oiled bowl, turn to coat, and cover with plastic wrap. Let rise in a warm place (70° to 80°F) until doubled in size, about 1 to 1½ hours.

Remove the dough from the bowl. Use it immediately or wrap it loosely in plastic wrap and refrigerate for up to 2 days. If chilled, let the dough stand at room temperature for 20 minutes before proceeding. Prepare the toppings.

To shape and bake

At least 20 minutes before baking, preheat the oven to 475°F. If using a baking stone or tiles, preheat the oven for 30 minutes with the stone or tiles on the lowest shelf. To make appetizer-size pizzette, cut the dough into quarters. Cut each piece of dough into sixths, pat into a ball, and press down with the heel of your palm to form a disc. With a rolling pin, roll each piece into a 4-inch round, or stretch the dough with your fingers. To make 6-inch pizzette, cut the dough into quarters, then cut each of these pieces into quarters and roll them into 6-inch rounds. Place on 3 oiled pizza pans or baking sheets. Top with toppings and let rise 20 minutes. If using a baking stone or tiles, place one pan on the preheated baking stone or tiles. Otherwise, place one pan on the middle shelf of the oven. Bake the 4-inch pizzette for 5 minutes and the 6-inch pizzette for 6 to 7 minutes, or until the crusts are crisp and browned on the bottom. Repeat to bake the remaining pizzette.

Untopped prebaked or partially baked crusts may be made ahead, then topped and reheated or baked. Most topped pizzette can be made in advance and reheated. The exceptions are those with cooked seafood, asparagus, squash, or broccoli. If the pizzette are made in advance, let cool and refrigerate, covered, for 1 day. Let frozen pizzette thaw. Reheat in a preheated 425°F oven until heated through, about 3 to 4 minutes.

Makes twenty-four 4-inch pizzette or sixteen 6-inch pizzette

Whole-Wheat Bran Pizzetta Dough

Substitute ¾ cup whole-wheat flour and ¼ cup wheat bran for 1 cup of unbleached all-purpose flour.

Four-Grain Pizzetta Dough

Substitute ½ cup whole-wheat flour and ¼ cup *each* corn-meal, barley flour, and rye flour for 1¼ cups unbleached all-purpose flour.

Buckwheat Pizzetta Dough

Substitute ¾ cup buckwheat flour for ¾ cup unbleached all-purpose flour. If the dough is sticky, knead in additional unbleached all-purpose flour.

Cornmeal Pizzetta Dough

Substitute ½ cup yellow, white, or blue cornmeal for ½ cup of the unbleached all-purpose flour.

Semolina Pizzetta Dough

Substitute ¾ cup semolina for ¾ cup of the unbleached all-purpose flour.

Saffron Pizzetta Dough

Add ⅛ teaspoon saffron threads to 1 cup boiling water. Let cool to 105° to 115°F, then substitute for the plain warm water. If desired, substitute ½ cup corn flour for ½ cup of the unbleached all-purpose flour to enhance the flavor and the golden color.

Rosemary-Sage Pizzetta Dough

Add 3 to 4 tablespoons mixed minced fresh rosemary and sage or thyme, chervil, parsley, tarragon, or basil to the Basic Pizzetta Dough or Whole-Wheat Bran Pizzetta Dough during mixing.

Whole-Wheat and Yogurt Pizzetta Dough

Instead of the 1 cup warm water, dissolve the yeast with the honey in ¼ cup warm water. Add ¾ cup plain low-fat yogurt. Substitute 1 cup whole-wheat flour for 1 cup of the unbleached all-purpose flour.

Sun-dried Tomato, Olive, and Semolina Pizzetta Dough

Substitute ½ cup semolina flour for ½ cup unbleached all-purpose flour and add 3 tablespoons minced pitted oil-cured black olives, 3 tablespoons snipped oil-packed sun-dried tomatoes, and 2 tablespoons minced mixed fresh thyme, basil, rosemary, or sage.

For a sweet pizzetta, it is easy to enhance a dough with honey or sugar, an egg, spices, citrus zest, and nuts.

Sweet Pizzetta Dough

2 teaspoons active dry yeast

3/4 cup warm water (105° to 115°F)

Pinch sugar plus 3 tablespoons honey or sugar

1 egg

1 teaspoon vanilla extract

2 teaspoons grated lemon zest (optional)

2 1/2 cups unbleached all-purpose flour

3/4 teaspoon salt

3 tablespoons butter or canola oil, room-temperature

Hand method

In a large bowl, sprinkle the yeast over the water and stir in the pinch of sugar. Let stand until dissolved and foamy, about 10 minutes. Mix in the honey or remaining sugar, egg, vanilla, lemon zest, 1 cup of the flour, the salt, and butter or oil, stirring with a wooden spoon until smooth. Gradually add the remaining flour 1/2 cup at a time, beating until the dough pulls away from the sides of the bowl. Turn out on a lightly floured board and knead until smooth and elastic, about 5 minutes.

Heavy-duty electric mixer method

In a heavy-duty electric mixer bowl, sprinkle the yeast over the water and stir in the pinch of sugar. Let stand until dissolved and foamy, about 10 minutes. Using the flat paddle attachment, mix in the honey or remaining sugar, egg, vanilla, lemon zest, 1 cup of the flour, the salt, and butter or oil, mixing until smooth. Gradually add the remaining flour 1/2 cup at a time and beat for 2 minutes, or until the dough clings together in a ball and is smooth and elastic. It is not necessary to knead by hand.

Food processor method

In a small bowl, sprinkle the yeast over the water and stir in the pinch of sugar. Let stand until dissolved and foamy, about 10 minutes. Place the flour and salt in a food processor with the metal blade attached. Process for 5 seconds. Add the honey or remaining sugar, egg, vanilla, lemon zest, and butter or oil to the yeast mixture and, with the machine running, pour this mixture through the feed tube and process until the dough clings together in a ball, about 30 seconds. Turn out on a lightly floured surface and knead for 1 or 2 minutes.

Place the dough in an oiled bowl, turn to coat, and cover with plastic wrap. Let rise in a warm place (70° to 80°F) until doubled in size, about 1 to 1½ hours.

Remove the dough from the bowl. Use it immediately or wrap it loosely in plastic wrap and refrigerate for up to 2 days. If chilled, let the dough stand at room temperature for 20 minutes before proceeding. Prepare the toppings.

To shape and bake

At least 20 minutes before baking, preheat the oven to 475°F. To make appetizer-size pizzette, cut the dough into quarters. Cut each piece of dough into sixths, pat into a ball, and press down with the heel of your palm to form a disc. With a rolling pin, roll each piece into a 4-inch round, or stretch the dough with your fingers. To make 6-inch pizzette, cut the dough into quarters, then cut each of these pieces into quarters and roll them into 6-inch rounds. Place on 3 oiled pizza pans or baking sheets. Add the toppings and let rise 20 minutes. If using a baking stone or tiles, place one pan on the preheated baking stone or tiles. Otherwise, place one pan on the middle shelf of the oven. Bake the 4-inch pizzette for 5 minutes and the 6-inch pizzette for 6 to 7 minutes, or until the crusts are crisp and browned on the bottom. Repeat to bake the remaining pizzette.

Makes twenty-four 4-inch pizzette or sixteen 6-inch pizzette

Cinnamon-Sugar Pizzetta Dough

In the Sweet Pizzetta Dough, omit the lemon zest and add 1 teaspoon ground cinnamon.

Orange Zest Pizzetta Dough

In the Sweet Pizzetta Dough, omit the lemon zest and add 1 tablespoon grated orange zest.

Chestnut Pizzetta Dough

In the Sweet Pizzetta Dough, instead of 2½ cups unbleached all-purpose flour, use 2¼ cups unbleached all-purpose flour and ¼ cup chestnut flour. Omit the lemon zest and add ¼ teaspoon ground nutmeg. Once the flour is added, mix in 8 finely chopped peeled roasted chestnuts or fresh-frozen steam-peeled chestnuts. Imported chestnut flour and fresh-frozen steam-peeled chestnuts are available through Chestnut Hill Orchards, 3300 Bee Cave Road, Austin, TX 78746; telephone 512-477-3020 in Texas, 800-745-3279 out of state.

garden
pizzette

PIZZETTE MARGHERITA

Named in 1889 in honor of Queen Margherita, these pizzette flaunt the green, white, and red colors of the *bandiera*—the Italian flag. The delicious essence of this simple combination depends on prime ingredients.

Basic or Cornmeal Pizzetta Dough

Olive oil, preferably extra-virgin, for brushing

2½ cups (10 ounces) shredded fresh mozzarella cheese, preferably imported and made in part from water buffalo milk

1½ pounds Roma (plum) tomatoes, chopped and well drained (about 3 cups)

2 tablespoons minced fresh basil or oregano

½ cup (2 ounces) freshly grated Parmesan cheese, preferably Parmigiano Reggiano

Small whole basil leaves for garnish

Prepare the dough. At least 20 minutes before baking, preheat the oven to 475°F. If using a baking stone or tiles, preheat the oven for 30 minutes with the stone or tiles on the bottom shelf of the oven.

Cut the dough into quarters, cut each piece of dough into sixths, and roll them into 4-inch rounds on a lightly floured surface. Or, cut the dough into quarters, then cut each of these pieces into quarters and roll them into 6-inch rounds on a lightly floured surface. Place on 3 oiled pizza pans or baking sheets and brush the rounds lightly with olive oil. Sprinkle the shredded cheese over the rounds. Cover with the tomatoes and sprinkle with basil or oregano and half the Parmesan cheese.

If using a baking stone or tiles, place one pan on the stone or tiles. Otherwise, place one pan on the middle shelf of the oven. Bake the 4-inch pizzette for 5 minutes and the 6-inch pizzette for 6 or 7 minutes, or until the crusts are crisp and browned on the bottom. Sprinkle with the remaining Parmesan cheese, garnish with the basil leaves, and serve immediately. Repeat to bake the remaining pizzette.

Makes twenty-four 4-inch or sixteen 6-inch pizzette

LEEK and GORGONZOLA PIZZETTE

Sweet caramelized leeks and onions meld with vibrant Gorgonzola in these savory bitefuls. These are great as appetizers, perhaps with a Provençal-style *vin gris*. Or serve as an accompaniment to grilled skirt steak or lamb kabobs, or pair with grilled salmon, swordfish, or scallop brochettes.

Four-Grain or Whole-Wheat Bran Pizzetta Dough

2 tablespoons olive oil, plus olive oil for brushing, preferably extra-virgin

2 large leeks, white and light green parts only, finely chopped (about 8 cups)

1 large yellow onion, chopped

4 ounces Gorgonzola cheese at room temperature

1½ cups (6 ounces) shredded Italian Fontina, Gruyère, or mozzarella cheese

Salt and freshly ground black pepper to taste

2 tablespoons minced fresh thyme, sage, or oregano

Prepare the dough. At least 20 minutes before baking, preheat the oven to 475°F. If using a baking stone or tiles, preheat the oven for 30 minutes with the stone or tiles on the bottom shelf of the oven.

In a large skillet or sauté pan over medium heat, heat the 2 tablespoons oil and sauté the leeks and onion until soft, about 7 to 8 minutes.

Cut the dough into quarters, cut each piece of dough into sixths, and roll them into 4-inch rounds on a lightly floured surface. Or, cut the dough into quarters, then cut each of these pieces into quarters and roll them into 6-inch rounds. Place on 3 oiled pizza pans or baking sheets and brush the rounds lightly with olive oil. Spread the Gorgonzola on the rounds and distribute the leek topping over them; sprinkle with the shredded cheese and season with salt and pepper.

If using a baking stone or tiles, place one pan on the stone or tiles. Otherwise, place one pan on the middle shelf of the oven. Bake the 4-inch pizzette for 5 minutes and the 6-inch pizzette for 6 or 7 minutes, or until the crusts are crisp and browned on the bottom. Sprinkle with the herbs and serve immediately. Repeat to bake the remaining pizzette.

Makes twenty-four 4-inch or sixteen 6-inch pizzette

BREAD BASKET PIZZETTE

For flavorsome breads to accompany a meal, fill a basket with two or three variations of herb- and olive-flecked pizzette. You can vary both the crust base and the toppings, for endless variety.

Herb and Sea Salt Pizzette

Basic; Sun-dried Tomato, Olive, and Semolina; Whole-Wheat Bran; or Rosemary-Sage Pizzetta Dough

Olive oil for brushing, plus 1 tablespoon olive oil, preferably extra-virgin

¼ cup minced fresh rosemary and sage

Coarse sea salt for sprinkling

Prepare the dough. At least 20 minutes before baking, preheat the oven to 475°F. If using a baking stone or tiles, preheat the oven for 30 minutes with the stone or tiles on the bottom shelf of the oven.

Cut the dough into quarters, cut each piece of dough into sixths, and roll them into 4-inch rounds on a lightly floured surface. Place on 3 oiled pizza pans or baking sheets and brush the dough lightly with olive oil.

Mix the herbs with the 1 tablespoon olive oil and distribute over the dough. Sprinkle lightly with the sea salt. If using a baking stone or tiles, place one pan on the stone or tiles. Otherwise, place one pan on the middle shelf of the oven. Bake the 4-inch pizzette for 5 minutes and the 6-inch pizzette for 6 to 7 minutes, or until the crusts are crisp and browned on the bottom. Serve immediately. Repeat to bake the remaining pizzette. If desired, the pizzette may be made ahead and reheated in a preheated 425°F oven for 2 to 3 minutes.

Makes twenty-four 4-inch pizzette

Olive and Lemon Variation

Prepare Basic, Four-Grain, or Whole-Wheat Bran Pizzetta Dough. Omit the herbs and sea salt in the preceding recipe and stud the dough with a mixture of 1 cup diced pitted oil-cured black olives and 2 teaspoons grated lemon zest. Bake as directed.

Garlic and Pecorino Romano Variation

Prepare the Basic, Four-Grain, or Whole-Wheat Bran Pizzetta Dough. Omit the herbs and sea salt in the main recipe and stud the dough with 6 finely slivered garlic cloves. Bake as directed. After baking, sprinkle the pizzette with ½ cup (2 ounces) grated pecorino romano cheese.

PIZZETTE GENOVESE

Pesto—the Genovese basil sauce that has become beloved world-wide—creates a zestful topping for cheese-crusted pizzette. As an alternate to pesto, try other spreads such as tapenade (see page 46) or sun-dried tomato and roasted garlic.

Basic, Whole-Wheat Bran, or
Cornmeal Pizzetta Dough

Pesto

2 cups packed fresh basil leaves

4 garlic cloves, smashed

⅓ cup pine nuts

⅓ cup olive oil, preferably
extra-virgin

½ cup (2 ounces) freshly grated
Parmesan, preferably Parmigiano
Reggiano, or part pecorino
romano cheese

Prepare the dough. At least 20 minutes before baking, preheat the oven to 475°F. If using a baking stone or tiles, preheat the oven for 30 minutes with the stone or tiles on the bottom shelf of the oven.

To make the pesto: In a blender or food processor, combine the basil, garlic, and pine nuts and purée until smooth. Add the oil and the ½ cup of grated cheese and blend until combined.

Cut the dough into quarters, cut each piece of dough into sixths, and roll them into 4-inch rounds on a lightly floured surface. Or, cut the piece of dough into quarters, then cut each of these pieces into quarters and roll them into 6-inch rounds. Place on 3 oiled pizza pans or baking sheets and prick the rounds in several places with the tines of a fork. Brush the rounds lightly with olive oil and sprinkle with 2½ cups shredded cheese.

If using a baking stone or tiles, place one pan on the stone or tiles. Otherwise, place one pan on the middle shelf of the oven. Bake the 4-inch pizzette for 5 minutes and the 6-inch pizzette for 6 or 7 minutes, or until the crusts are crisp and browned on the bottom. Spoon on the pesto, sprinkle with the ¼ cup Parmesan cheese, garnish with the pine nuts or basil leaves, and serve immediately. Repeat to bake the remaining pizzette. If desired, untopped crusts may be reheated in a preheated 425°F oven for 2 to 3 minutes and then topped.

Olive oil, preferably extra virgin, for brushing

2½ cups (10 ounces) shredded mozzarella or Monterey jack cheese

¼ cup freshly grated Parmesan, preferably Parmigiano Reggiano

Pine nuts or small basil leaves for garnish

Makes twenty-four 4-inch or sixteen 6-inch pizzette

MUSHROOM, LEEK, and GOAT CHEESE PIZZETTE

A rustic buckwheat or four-grain crust makes a savory base for a succulent topping of mushrooms, caramelized leeks, and creamy goat cheese. Serve as a delightful first course or accompaniment to grilled chicken breasts coated with Dijon mustard and herbs, green beans, and lemon ice mounded in zigzag-cut lemon half shells.

Buckwheat or Four-Grain
Pizzetta Dough

2 tablespoons olive oil, plus olive oil for brushing, preferably extra-virgin

2 leeks, finely chopped (white part only), or 2 sweet white onions, chopped

12 ounces white or brown mushrooms, sliced

8 ounces fresh mild goat cheese or natural cream cheese at room temperature, or crumbled feta cheese

1½ cups (6 ounces) shredded Jarlsberg, Gruyère, or Monterey jack cheese

3 tablespoons pine nuts

Small fresh basil, tarragon, or oregano leaves

Prepare the dough. At least 20 minutes before baking, preheat the oven to 475°F. If using a baking stone or tiles, preheat the oven for 30 minutes with the stone or tiles on the bottom shelf of the oven.

In a large skillet or sauté pan over medium heat, heat 1 tablespoon oil and sauté the leeks until soft, about 7 to 8 minutes; transfer to a bowl. Heat the remaining 1 tablespoon oil in the same pan and sauté the mushrooms over medium-high heat until glazed, about 2 minutes; add to the leeks.

Cut the dough into quarters, cut each piece of dough into sixths, and roll them into 4-inch rounds on a lightly floured surface. Or, cut the dough into quarters, then cut each of these pieces into quarters and roll them into 6-inch rounds. Place on 3 oiled pizza pans or baking sheets and brush the rounds lightly with olive oil.

Spread the dough with the goat or cream cheese or sprinkle with the feta and spoon the sautéed vegetables over. Top with the shredded cheese and nuts. If using a baking stone or tiles, place one pan on the stone or tiles. Otherwise, place one pan on the middle shelf of the oven. Bake the 4-inch pizzette for 5 minutes and the 6-inch pizzette for 6 or 7 minutes, or until the crusts are crisp and browned on the bottom. Sprinkle with herbs and serve immediately. Repeat to bake the remaining pizzette.

Makes twenty-four 4-inch or sixteen 6-inch pizzette

Variation
Add 3 ounces julienned prosciutto to the sautéed vegetables before sprinkling over the dough.

GOLDEN SQUASH and RED PEPPER PIZZETTE

Red, green, and gold vegetables emblazen pizzette for an appealing vegetarian-style appetizer or entrée. This is an excellent way to utilize any type of summer squash when the harvest becomes prolific.

Four-Grain, Cornmeal, or Basic Pizzetta Dough

6 yellow straight-neck or crook-neck squash, thinly sliced

Salt for sprinkling

2 sweet white onions, thinly sliced

Olive oil for coating and brushing, preferably extra-virgin

2 garlic cloves, minced

1 bunch green onions with tops, chopped

1 red bell pepper, halved, seeded, deribbed, and cut into strips (optional)

¼ cup minced fresh oregano or basil

¼ teaspoon freshly ground black pepper

Prepare the dough and preheat the oven to 350°F. If using a baking stone or tiles, place the stone or tiles on the bottom shelf of the oven while preheating.

Sprinkle the squash with salt, place in a colander set over a bowl, and let drain for 20 minutes to eliminate excess moisture. Rinse thoroughly under cold water and pat dry with paper towels. Coat the squash and white onion slices lightly with olive oil and arrange on a baking sheet; scatter the garlic over. Bake until tender, about 20 minutes. Mix in the green onions, optional bell pepper, oregano or basil, and pepper.

Increase the oven heat to 475°F. Cut the dough into quarters, cut each piece of dough into sixths, and roll them into 4-inch rounds on a lightly floured surface. Or, cut the dough into quarters, then cut each of these pieces into quarters and roll them into 6-inch rounds. Place on 3 oiled pizza pans or baking sheets and brush the rounds lightly with olive oil. Sprinkle with the shredded and crumbled cheeses and top with the vegetable mixture.

If using a baking stone or tiles, place one pan on the stone or tiles. Otherwise, place one pan on the middle shelf of the oven. Bake the 4-inch pizzette for 5 minutes and the 6-inch pizzette for 6 or 7 minutes, or until the crusts are crisp and browned on the bottom. Sprinkle with the grated cheese and whole or minced herbs and serve immediately. Repeat to bake the remaining pizzette.

Makes twenty-four 4-inch or sixteen 6-inch pizzette

1½ cups (6 ounces) shredded Monterey jack or Bel Paese cheese

2 cups (8 ounces) crumbled feta cheese

½ cup (2 ounces) freshly grated Parmesan, dry jack, or Asiago cheese

Whole or minced fresh oregano or basil leaves for garnish

GREEK ISLAND PIZZETTE

Feta cheese, tomatoes, and pine nuts imbue these vegetable pizzette with a Greek island flavor. Let them prelude a guest dinner featuring grilled lamb or shrimp kabobs and pine nut pilaf. Finish off with melon, Muscat grapes, and halvah.

Basic, Four-Grain, Whole-Wheat Bran, or Sun-dried Tomato, Olive, and Semolina Pizzetta Dough

1½ pounds fresh broccoli, cut into florets, or two 10-ounce packages frozen artichoke hearts

2 tablespoons olive oil, plus olive oil for brushing, preferably extra-virgin

8 ounces feta cheese, crumbled (2 cups)

4 green onions with tops, chopped

3 Roma (plum) tomatoes, chopped

¼ cup pine nuts

4 ounces thinly slivered kasseri, Asiago, or dry jack cheese

2 tablespoons minced fresh oregano or chives

Prepare the dough. At least 20 minutes before baking, preheat the oven to 475°F. If using a baking stone or tiles, preheat the oven for 30 minutes with the stone or tiles on the bottom shelf of the oven.

In a medium saucepan, cook the broccoli or artichokes in boiling salted water until crisp-tender, about 5 to 7 minutes; rinse in cold water and drain. Cut the vegetables into small pieces and toss in the 2 tablespoons oil.

Cut the dough into quarters, cut each piece of dough into sixths, and roll them into 4-inch rounds on a lightly floured surface. Or, cut the dough into quarters, then cut each of the pieces into quarters and roll them into 6-inch rounds. Place on 3 oiled pizza pans or baking pans and brush the rounds lightly with oil, and sprinkle with the crumbled cheese. Combine the broccoli or artichokes, green onions, and tomatoes, and distribute over the top. Sprinkle with nuts.

If using a baking stone or tiles, place one pan on the stone or tiles. Otherwise, place one pan on the middle shelf of the oven. Bake the 4-inch pizzette for 5 minutes and the 6-inch pizzette for 6 or 7 minutes, or until the crusts are crisp and browned on the bottom. Top each pizzetta with shavings of cheese, sprinkle with mixed herbs, and serve immediately. Repeat to bake the remaining pizzette.

Makes twenty-four 4-inch or sixteen 6-inch pizzette

RATATOUILLE PIZZETTE

Ratatouille comes in countless variations: mild, spicy, chunky, and fine. Here, in the form of a vibrant relish, it tops pizzette for winning appetizers or vegetarian entrées. These also go well with lamb dishes.

Four-Grain, Rosemary-Sage, Cornmeal, or Whole-Wheat Bran Pizzetta Dough

Ratatouille

3 zucchini, diced

3 Japanese eggplants, diced

Salt for sprinkling

2 tablespoons olive oil, preferably extra-virgin

3 shallots, minced, or 1 yellow onion, chopped

2 garlic cloves, minced

1 small red bell pepper, seeded, deribbed, and diced

2 tablespoons minced fresh flat-leaf (Italian) parsley

2 tablespoons minced fresh basil or oregano

Salt and freshly ground black pepper to taste

Prepare the dough. At least 20 minutes before baking, preheat the oven to 475°F. If using a baking stone or tiles, preheat the oven for 30 minutes with the stone or tiles on the bottom shelf of the oven. Sprinkle the zucchini and eggplants lightly with salt and let sit in a colander for 30 minutes; rinse thoroughly and pat dry with paper towels.

In a large skillet or sauté pan over medium-high heat, heat the oil and sauté the shallots or onion until translucent, about 3 minutes. Add the zucchini, eggplants, and garlic, and sauté until crisp-tender, about 3 to 4 minutes. Add the bell pepper, parsley, and basil or oregano and heat through. Season with salt and pepper and set aside.

Divide the dough into quarters, cut each piece of dough into sixths, and roll them into 4-inch rounds on a lightly floured surface. Or, cut the dough into quarters, then cut each of these pieces into quarters and roll them into 6-inch rounds. Place on 3 cornmeal-sprinkled or oiled pizza pans or baking sheets and brush the rounds lightly with olive oil. Sprinkle with the shredded cheese and top with the ratatouille.

If using a baking stone or tiles, place one pan on the stone or tiles. Otherwise, place one pan on the middle shelf of the oven. Bake the 4-inch pizzette for 5 minutes and the 6-inch pizzette for 6 or 7 minutes, or until the crusts are crisp and browned on the bottom. Sprinkle with the grated cheese and whole or minced herbs. Serve immediately. Repeat to bake the remaining pizzette.

Makes twenty-four 4-inch or sixteen 6-inch pizzette

Olive oil for brushing, preferably extra-virgin

2 cups (8 ounces) shredded Gruyère, Jarlsberg, or Port-Salut cheese

½ cup (2 ounces) freshly grated Parmesan (preferably Parmigiano Reggiano), dry jack, or Asiago cheese

Whole or minced fresh basil or oregano leaves for garnish

ASPARAGUS and GREEN ONION PIZZETTE

These springtime pizzette flaunt asparagus and first-of-the-season peas on a bed of goat cheese.

Basic, Cornmeal, or Buckwheat Pizzetta Dough

1 tablespoon olive oil, plus olive oil for coating and brushing, preferably extra-virgin

1 bunch green onions with tops, chopped

1½ pounds asparagus, tough stems discarded and stalks cut into ⅜ inch-thick diagonal slices

1½ pounds fresh green peas, shelled, or 1½ cups thawed frozen green peas

6 ounces fresh mild goat cheese at room temperature or feta cheese, crumbled

Salt and freshly ground black pepper to taste

1½ cups (6 ounces) shredded Gruyère, Jarlsberg, or mozzarella cheese

3 tablespoons minced fresh chives or tarragon

Prepare the dough. At least 20 minutes before baking, preheat the oven to 475°F. If using a baking stone or tiles, preheat the oven for 30 minutes with the stone or tiles on the bottom shelf of the oven.

In a medium skillet or sauté pan over medium heat, heat the 1 tablespoon oil and sauté the onions until translucent, about 3 to 4 minutes. Separately steam or blanch the asparagus for about 3 to 5 minutes and the peas for 2 to 3 minutes, or until crisp-tender, rinsing them in cold water to retain their color; drain the vegetables well and coat them with olive oil.

Cut the dough into quarters, cut each piece of dough into sixths, and roll them into 4-inch rounds on a lightly floured surface. Or, cut the dough into quarters, then cut each of these pieces into quarters and roll them into 6-inch rounds. Place on 3 oiled pizza pans or baking sheets and brush the rounds lightly with olive oil. Spread the goat cheese over the rounds, or sprinkle with the feta, and top with the asparagus, peas, and green onions. Season with salt and pepper and sprinkle with the shredded cheese.

If using a baking stone or tiles, place one pan on the stone or tiles. Otherwise, place one pan on the middle shelf of the oven. Bake the 4-inch pizzette for 5 minutes and the 6-inch pizzette for 6 or 7 minutes, or until the crusts are crisp and browned on the bottom. Sprinkle with the herbs and serve immediately. Repeat to bake the remaining pizzette.

Makes twenty-four 4-inch or sixteen 6-inch pizzette

SUN-DRIED TOMATO and OLIVE PIZZETTE

A flavor-packed topping of caramelized onions, sun-dried tomatoes, herbs, and cheese makes these chewy pizzette perfect for a Mediterranean repast.

Basic, Whole-Wheat Bran, or Cornmeal Pizzetta Dough

2 tablespoons olive oil, plus olive oil for brushing, preferably extra-virgin

2 large sweet red or white onions, chopped

3 green onions with tops, chopped

3 tablespoons minced mixed fresh thyme, basil, sage, and rosemary

1 cup oil-cured black olives, pitted and chopped

1½ cups oil-cured sun-dried tomatoes, drained and chopped

2½ cups (10 ounces) shredded Italian Fontina or Monterey jack cheese

¼ cup chopped pistachios

¼ cup freshly grated Parmesan, preferably Parmigiano Reggiano, or pecorino romano cheese

Small basil or sage leaves for garnish

Prepare the dough. At least 20 minutes before baking, preheat the oven to 475°F. If using a baking stone or tiles, preheat the oven for 30 minutes with the stone or tiles on the bottom shelf of the oven.

In a large skillet or sauté pan over medium heat, heat the 2 tablespoons of oil and sauté the two kinds of onions until translucent, about 7 minutes; transfer to a bowl. Let cool and mix in the herbs, olives, and sun-dried tomatoes.

Cut the dough into quarters, cut each piece of dough into sixths, and roll them into 4-inch rounds on a lightly floured surface. Or, cut the dough into quarters, then cut each of these pieces into quarters and roll them into 6-inch rounds. Place on 3 oiled pizza pans or baking sheets and brush the rounds lightly with olive oil. Sprinkle the shredded cheese over the dough and distribute the olive mixture over it. Sprinkle with pistachios.

If using a baking stone or tiles, place one pan on the stone or tiles. Otherwise, place one pan on the middle shelf of the oven. Bake the 4-inch pizzette for 5 minutes and the 6-inch pizzette for 6 or 7 minutes, or until the crusts are crisp and browned on the bottom. Sprinkle with the remaining ¼ cup Parmesan cheese, garnish with the herb leaves, and serve immediately. Repeat to bake the remaining pizzette.

Makes twenty-four 4-inch or sixteen 6-inch pizzette

SANTA FE TRICOLOR PIZZETTE

A trio of peppers lends brilliant colors to these zestful pizzette. Roasting brings out a sweetness in the peppers and lends a smoky overtone. It also allows you to peel off the skin easily. You might round out the menu with a chili or black bean stew; a jícama, orange, and avocado salad; and coffee ice cream floats.

Cornmeal, Whole-Wheat Bran, or Basic Pizzetta Dough

2 tablespoons olive oil, plus olive oil for brushing, preferably extra-virgin

½ teaspoon ground cumin

1 green, 1 yellow, and 3 red bell peppers, roasted, peeled, seeded, and chopped (see next page)

1 red onion, chopped

Salt and freshly ground black pepper to taste

6 tablespoons minced fresh cilantro

2½ cups (10 ounces) shredded jalapeño jack or regular Monterey jack cheese

Guacamole

Prepare the dough. At least 20 minutes before baking, preheat the oven to 475°F. If using a baking stone or tiles, preheat the oven for 30 minutes with the stone or tiles on the bottom shelf of the oven.

In a large skillet or sauté pan over medium heat, heat 1 tablespoon of the oil with the cumin and sauté the peppers and onion until soft, about 5 minutes. Stir in the salt, pepper, and half of the cilantro.

Divide the dough into quarters, cut each piece of dough into sixths, and roll into 4-inch rounds on a lightly floured surface. Or, cut the dough into quarters, then cut each of these pieces into quarters and roll them to make 6-inch rounds. Place on 3 oiled pizza pans or baking sheets and brush the dough lightly with olive oil. Sprinkle the cheese over the rounds and distribute the pepper and onion mixture over the dough.

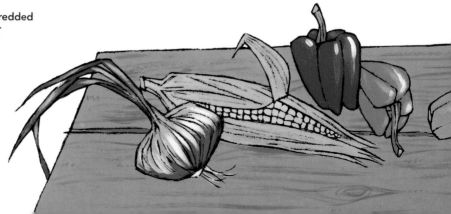

If using a baking stone or tiles, place one pan on the stone or tiles. Otherwise, place one pan on the middle shelf of the oven. Bake the 4-inch pizzette for 5 minutes and the 6-inch pizzette for 6 or 7 minutes, or until the crusts are crisp and browned on the bottom. Top each pizzetta with a spoonful of guacamole and sprinkle with the cilantro. Serve immediately. Repeat to bake the remaining pizzette.

Makes twenty-four 4-inch or sixteen 6-inch pizzette

Variation
Add 1 chorizo (about 5 ounces), removed from casing, cooked, crumbled, and drained, to the pepper mixture.

Roasting and Peeling Peppers
Place whole peppers over a charcoal fire, directly in a gas flame, or under a preheated broiler. Roast, turning, until the skin is charred all over. Transfer to a paper bag, loosely close the bag, and let stand for 10 minutes. Peel the charred skin from the peppers. Cut the peppers in half and remove the seeds and ribs.

SALAD PIZZETTE

Crisp pizzetta crusts topped with mixed greens and grapes are like little salads to eat out of hand.

Basic, Whole-Wheat Bran, or Cornmeal Pizzetta Dough

Olive oil for brushing, plus ⅓ cup olive oil, preferably extra-virgin

2½ cups (10 ounces) freshly shredded aged white Cheddar, Gruyère, or Port-Salut cheese

½ cup (2 ounces) freshly grated Parmesan, preferably Parmigiano Reggiano or part pecorino romano cheese

3 tablespoons balsamic vinegar

2 teaspoons Dijon mustard

Salt and freshly ground black pepper to taste

6 cups torn mixed small salad greens, such as red oak leaf lettuce, radicchio, mâche, frisée, and butter lettuce

1 cup red or green seedless grapes or small cherry tomatoes, halved

¼ cup blanched slivered almonds or pine nuts, toasted (see next page)

Prepare the dough. At least 20 minutes before baking, preheat the oven to 475°F. If using a baking stone or tiles, preheat the oven for 30 minutes with the stone or tiles on the bottom shelf of the oven.

Divide the dough into quarters, cut each piece of dough into sixths, and roll them into 4-inch rounds on a lightly floured surface. Or, cut the dough into quarters, then cut each piece into quarters and roll them into 6-inch rounds. Place on 3 oiled pizza pans or baking sheets and brush the dough with olive oil, and sprinkle the cheeses over the dough.

If using a baking stone or tiles, place one pan on the stone or tiles. Otherwise, place one pan on the middle shelf of the oven. Bake the 4-inch pizzette for 5 minutes and the 6-inch pizzette for 6 to 7 minutes, or until the crusts are crisp and browned on the bottom.

Meanwhile, in a bowl or a jar with a lid, combine the vinegar, mustard, salt, and pepper. Whisk or shake to blend, add the oil, and whisk or shake to emulsify. Toss with the salad greens and grapes or tomatoes.

Spoon on the salad onto the pizzette, scatter the nuts over it, and serve immediately. Repeat to bake the remaining pizzette. If desired, the crusts may be baked in advance and reheated in a 425°F oven for 2 or 3 minutes before topping.

Makes twenty-four 4-inch or sixteen 6-inch pizzette

Toasting Nuts

Preheat the oven to 325° F. Place the nuts in a baking pan and bake for 8 to 10 minutes, or until lightly browned.

chicken, seafood & other savory pizzette

PROSCIUTTO and FONTINA PIZZETTE

Croque monsieur, a classic sandwich from Parisian cafés, inspired this simple and delectable open-face snack with Italian flair. Accompany with bowls of cornichons, Mediterranean olives, and cherry tomatoes.

Basic, Whole-Wheat Bran, or Cornmeal Pizzetta Dough

Olive oil for brushing

2 tablespoons Dijon mustard

2½ cups (10 ounces) shredded Italian Fontina or Gruyère

8 ounces thinly sliced prosciutto or Black Forest ham, cut into ½-inch-wide strips

Chopped arugula or watercress leaves

Prepare the dough. At least 20 minutes before baking, preheat the oven to 475°F. If using a baking stone or tiles, preheat the oven for 30 minutes with the stone or tiles on the bottom shelf of the oven.

Cut the dough into quarters, cut each piece of dough into sixths, and roll them into 4-inch rounds on a lightly floured board. Or, cut the dough into quarters, then cut each of these pieces into quarters and roll them into 6-inch rounds. Place on 3 oiled pizza pans or baking sheets. Brush the rounds lightly with olive oil and spread lightly with mustard. Sprinkle the cheese over the rounds and top with the prosciutto or ham.

If using a baking stone or tiles, place one pan on the stone or tiles. Otherwise, place one pan on the middle shelf of the oven. Bake the 4-inch pizzette for 5 minutes and the 6-inch pizzette for 6 or 7 minutes, or until the crusts are crisp and lightly browned on the bottom. Garnish with herbs and serve immediately. Repeat to bake the remaining pizzette.

Makes twenty-four 4-inch or sixteen 6-inch pizzette

POTATO and ARUGULA PIZZETTE

The Yukon Gold variety of potatoes retain their lovely yellow hue after baking. Arrange the slices in a petal-like pattern atop the pizzette and adorn with chive petals or sage blossoms, if available. Let these accompany grilled specialty sausages or mustard-glazed pork tenderloin and sugar snap peas.

Basic or Cornmeal Pizzetta Dough

6 medium-large unpeeled Yukon Gold potatoes, sliced ³/₈ inch thick

Olive oil for brushing, plus 2 tablespoons olive oil, preferably extra-virgin

Salt and freshly ground black pepper to taste

6 ounces ricotta or fresh mild goat cheese at room temperature

1 bunch green onions with tops, chopped

4 ounces thinly sliced pancetta, cut into julienne

3 tablespoons minced fresh thyme, oregano, sage, or a combination

1½ cups (6 ounces) shredded Gruyère, Jarlsberg, or Samsoe cheese

Chopped arugula leaves

Chive or sage blossoms (optional)

Prepare the dough. At least 20 minutes before baking, preheat the oven to 475°F. If using a baking stone or tiles, preheat the oven for 30 minutes with the stone or tiles on the bottom shelf of the oven.

Place the potatoes on an oiled baking sheet and brush the potatoes with oil. Season with salt and pepper. Bake in the preheated oven for 10 minutes, or until just barely tender; let cool.

Cut the dough into quarters, cut each piece of dough into sixths, and roll them into 4-inch rounds on a lightly floured surface. Or, cut the dough into quarters, then cut each of these pieces into quarters and roll them into 6-inch rounds. Place on 3 oiled pizza pans or baking pans and brush the dough rounds lightly with olive oil. Spread the ricotta or goat cheese over the dough and top with the green onions, overlapping potato slices, pancetta, and chopped herbs. Sprinkle with the shredded cheese.

If using a baking stone or tiles, place one pan on the stone or tiles. Otherwise, place one pan on the middle shelf of the oven. Bake the 4-inch pizzette for 5 minutes and the 6-inch pizzette for 6 or 7 minutes, or until the crusts are crisp and lightly browned on the bottom. Top with the chopped arugula and optional petals or blossoms and serve immediately. Repeat to bake the remaining pizzette.

Makes twenty-four 4-inch or sixteen 6-inch pizzette

PIZZETTE NIÇOISE

The marvelous outdoor market in Nice inspires these zesty pizzette. Vendors there sell huge chickpea flour pancakes called *socca*, and an endless variety of seafood and olives. The topping for these golden doughs are available in any American supermarket.

Cornmeal, Semolina, or
Saffron Pizzetta Dough

Tapenade

1½ cups oil-cured black or
green olives, pitted and
chopped

⅓ cup firmly packed fresh
basil leaves

3 tablespoons chopped fresh
flat-leaf (Italian) parsley

3 anchovy fillets

2 tablespoons capers, rinsed
and drained

3 garlic cloves, minced

2 tablespoons extra-virgin
olive oil

1 tablespoon fresh lemon juice

Salt and freshly ground black
pepper to taste

Prepare the dough. At least 20 minutes before baking, preheat the oven to 475°F. If using a baking stone or tiles, preheat the oven for 30 minutes with the stone or tiles on the bottom shelf of the oven.

To make the tapenade: In a blender or food processor, combine the olives, basil, parsley, anchovies, capers, garlic, and olive oil and purée until smooth. Add the lemon juice, salt, and pepper. Set aside.

Cut the dough into quarters, cut each piece of dough into sixths, and roll them into 4-inch rounds on a lightly floured surface. Or, cut the dough into quarters, then cut each of these pieces into quarters and roll them into 6-inch rounds. Place on 3 oiled pizza pans or baking sheets and brush the rounds lightly with olive oil, spread with tapenade, and scatter the onion and peppers over them.

If using a baking stone or tiles, place one pan on the stone or tiles. Otherwise, place one pan on the middle shelf of the oven. Bake the 4-inch pizzette for 5 minutes and the 6-inch pizzette for 6 or 7 minutes or until the crusts are crisp and browned on the bottom. Sprinkle with the grated cheese and herbs and serve immediately. Repeat to bake the remaining pizzette.

Makes twenty-four 4-inch or sixteen 6-inch pizzette

Olive oil, preferably extra-virgin, for brushing

1 large red onion, chopped

2 red bell peppers, roasted, peeled, seeded, and chopped (see page 39)

¼ cup freshly grated pecorino romano or Parmesan cheese, preferably Parmigiano Reggiano

Minced fresh basil or oregano sprigs

SHRIMP PIZZETTE with MANGO SALSA

A refreshing salsa tops shrimp on these seafood pizzettes. Yogurt cheese is a low-fat substitute for traditional cream cheese.

Basic, Cornmeal, or Sun-dried Tomato, Olive, and Semolina Pizzetta Dough

Mango Salsa

1 mango, peeled, seeded, and diced

2 tablespoons chopped red onion

2 tablespoons minced fresh cilantro

2 tablespoons fresh lime or lemon juice

1 tablespoon minced fresh hot chili or to taste

Salt to taste

Olive oil, preferably extra-virgin, for brushing

Prepare the dough. At least 20 minutes before baking, preheat the oven to 475°F. If using a baking stone or tiles, preheat the oven for 30 minutes with the stone or tiles on the bottom shelf of the oven. To prepare the salsa: In a small bowl combine the mango, onion, cilantro, lime or lemon juice, chili, and salt, and set aside.

Cut the dough into quarters, cut each piece of dough into sixths, and roll them into 4-inch rounds on a lightly floured surface. Or, cut the dough into quarters, then cut each of these pieces into quarters and roll them into 6-inch rounds. Place on 3 oiled pizza pans or baking sheets. Prick the rounds all over with a fork and brush the dough with olive oil.

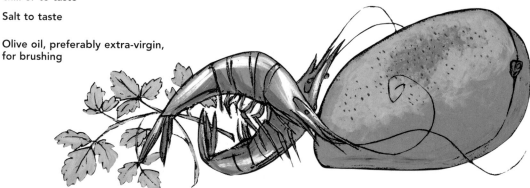

If using a baking stone or tiles, place one pan on the stone or tiles. Otherwise, place one pan on the middle shelf of the oven. Bake for 4 minutes, or until the crusts are firm and lightly browned. Spread with the cheese, leaving a border around the edge. Sprinkle with the onion, shrimp, and shredded or sliced cheese.

Return to the oven for 1 to 2 minutes, or until the crusts are crisp and browned on the bottom. Top each pizzetta with a spoonful of mango salsa, garnish with the cilantro, and serve immediately. Repeat to bake the remaining pizzette. If desired, the untopped crusts may be baked in advance, then topped and heated.

Makes twenty-four 4-inch or sixteen 6-inch pizzette

1¾ cups yogurt cheese (see below), or 12 ounces natural cream cheese, at room temperature

¾ cup finely chopped sweet red onion

12 ounces cooked small shrimp

1½ cups (6 ounces) shredded Monterey jack cheese or sliced Teleme cheese

Minced fresh cilantro for garnish

Yogurt Cheese

Spoon 4 cups (2 pounds) plain yogurt, made without gelatin, into a strainer lined with cheese-cloth and placed over a bowl. Cover and refrigerate for 12 to 24 hours, or until thickened. Discard the whey or use it for baking or in a sauce or soup. Makes 1¾ cups.

PEPERONATA PIZZETTE

Peperonata—a stew of red and yellow peppers, tomato, and onion—makes a splendid pizzetta topping to combine with tangy feta and spicy sausage. On a summer evening, serve these with sangría and an avocado and tomato salad for an informal repast. Or, for a company dinner, serve as a first course with grilled herb-coated chicken or game hens or lamb kabobs.

Mix and knead the dough, then set it aside to rise. Meanwhile, to make the peperonata: In a large saucepan, heat the oil over medium heat and cook the peppers, tomatoes, onion, and cumin for a few minutes; reduce the heat to low and cook, covered, for 1 hour, stirring occasionally. Season with vinegar, salt, and pepper, and cook over medium heat, uncovered, until all the liquid has evaporated. Let cool.

At least 20 minutes before baking, preheat the oven to 475°F. If using a baking stone or tiles, preheat the oven for 30 minutes with the stone or tiles on the bottom shelf of the oven.

Four-Grain, Rosemary-Sage, Cornmeal, or Whole-Wheat Bran Pizzetta Dough

Peperonata

3 tablespoons olive oil, preferably extra-virgin

2 jalapeño chilies, seeded and minced

2 red bell peppers, halved, seeded, deribbed, and cut into strips

2 yellow bell peppers, halved, seeded, deribbed, and cut into strips

6 large Roma (plum) tomatoes, chopped

1 large yellow onion, chopped

1 teaspoon ground cumin

1 tablespoon red wine vinegar

Salt and freshly ground black pepper to taste

Remove the sausage meat from its casing and crumble it. In a medium skillet or sauté pan, cook the sausage over medium-high heat until thoroughly browned. Drain the sausage meat and stir it into the peperonata when the dough has doubled.

Cut the dough into quarters, cut each piece of dough into sixths, and roll them into 4-inch rounds on a lightly floured surface. Or, cut the dough into quarters, then cut each of these pieces into quarters and roll them into 6-inch rounds. Place on oiled pizza pans or baking sheets and brush the rounds lightly with olive oil. Sprinkle the crumbled or diced cheese over the rounds and cover with the peperonata, parsley, or basil, and grated cheese.

If using a baking stone or tiles, place one pan on the stone or tiles. Otherwise, place one pan on the middle shelf of the oven. Bake the 4-inch pizzette for 5 minutes and the 6-inch pizzette for 6 or 7 minutes, or until the crusts are crisp and browned on the bottom. Serve immediately. Repeat to bake the remaining pizzette.

Makes twenty-four 4-inch or sixteen 6-inch pizzette

3 chicken or pork Italian-style sausages (about 12 ounces)

Olive oil for brushing, preferably extra-virgin

1 cup (4 ounces) crumbled feta cheese or diced Monterey jack or muenster cheese

1/2 cup minced fresh flat-leaf (Italian) parsley or basil

1/2 cup (2 ounces) freshly grated Parmesan (preferably Parmigiano Reggiano) or pecorino romano cheese

BUCKWHEAT PIZZETTE with CAVIAR

Designed for a party, these elegant pizzette call for champagne.

Buckwheat or Basic Pizzetta Dough

Olive oil, preferably extra-virgin, for brushing

12 ounces natural cream cheese at room temperature

1 cup minced sweet red onion

8 ounces red or black caviar

3 hard-cooked eggs, yolks sieved and whites chopped

Minced fresh chives or dill for garnish

Prepare the dough. At least 20 minutes before baking, preheat the oven to 475° F. If using a baking stone or tiles, preheat the oven for 30 minutes with the stone or tiles on the bottom shelf of the oven.

Divide the dough into quarters, cut each piece of dough into sixths, and roll them into 4-inch rounds on a lightly floured board. Or cut the dough into quarters, cut each of these pieces into quarters and roll them into 6-inch rounds. Place on 3 oiled pizza pans or baking sheets. Prick the dough all over with a fork and brush the dough lightly with olive oil.

If using a baking stone or tiles, place one pan on the stone or tiles. Otherwise, place one pan on the middle shelf of the oven. Bake the 4-inch pizzette for 5 minutes and the 6-inch pizzette for 6 or 7 minutes or until the crusts are crisp and browned on the bottom. Spread with the cheese. Scatter the onion over. Dollop the caviar in the center and place a spoonful each of egg yolk and egg white alongside. Garnish with the chives or dill and serve immediately. Repeat to bake the remaining pizzette. If desired, the untopped crusts may be baked in advance, then topped and reheated in a preheated 425°F oven for 2 to 3 minutes.

Makes twenty-four 4-inch or sixteen 6-inch pizzette

SMOKED SALMON PIZZETTE with GOAT CHEESE

For a party celebration, smoked fish and goat cheese top pizzette to serve with champagne as a gala prelude to a fête.

Basic, Buckwheat, or Cornmeal Pizzetta Dough

Olive oil, preferably extra-virgin, for brushing

12 ounces fresh mild goat cheese, mascarpone, or natural cream cheese at room temperature

½ cup finely chopped sweet red onion

8 ounces thinly sliced smoked salmon or flaked smoked trout

3 tablespoons capers, drained

Minced fresh dill or chives for garnish

Prepare the dough. At least 20 minutes before baking, preheat the oven to 475°F. If using a baking stone or tiles, preheat the oven for 30 minutes with the stone or tiles on the bottom shelf of the oven.

Cut the dough into quarters, cut each piece of dough into sixths, and roll them into 4-inch rounds on a lightly floured surface. Or, cut the dough into quarters, then cut each of these pieces into quarters and roll them into 6-inch rounds. Place on 3 oiled pizza pans or baking sheets. Prick the rounds with a fork and brush the dough lightly with olive oil.

If using a baking stone or tiles, place one pan on the stone or tiles. Otherwise, place one pan on the middle shelf of the oven. Bake the rounds for 4 minutes, or until the crusts are firm.

Spread the crusts with the cheese, leaving a border around the edge, and sprinkle with the onion.

Return to a preheated 425° F oven for 1 to 2 minutes, or until the crusts are crisp and browned on the bottom. Top each pizzetta with the fish, capers, and minced dill or chives, and serve immediately. Repeat to bake the remaining pizzette. If desired the untopped crusts may be baked in advance, then topped and baked.

Makes twenty-four 4-inch or sixteen 6-inch pizzette

ITALIAN SAUSAGE and ZUCCHINI PIZZETTE

Choose hot or mild sausage to suit your whim for these Mediterranean-style appetizers. Serve them with an orange, olive, and arugula salad, fettuccine with pesto, and biscotti.

Four-Grain, Whole-Wheat Bran, or Cornmeal Pizzetta Dough

4 mild or hot Italian sausage (about 1 pound)

2 tablespoons olive oil, plus olive oil for brushing, preferably extra-virgin

6 green onions with tops, chopped

4 zucchini, thinly sliced

8 ounces ricotta cheese

1½ cups (6 ounces) shredded Italian Fontina, Monterey jack, or fresh mozzarella cheese

2 tablespoons minced fresh basil or oregano

Prepare the dough. At least 20 minutes before baking, preheat the oven to 475°F. If using a baking stone or tiles, preheat the oven for 30 minutes with the stone or tiles on the bottom shelf of the oven.

Meanwhile, in a medium saucepan, cook the sausage in barely simmering water to cover for 15 minutes; let cool, then slice. In a large skillet or sauté pan over medium heat, heat the 2 tablespoons oil and sauté the onions and zucchini until crisp-tender, about 3 to 4 minutes; combine with the sausage. Set aside.

Cut the dough into quarters, cut each piece of dough into sixths, and roll them into 4-inch rounds on a floured surface. Or, cut the dough into quarters, then cut each of these pieces into quarters and roll them into 6-inch rounds. Place on 3 oiled pizza pans or baking sheets and brush the rounds lightly with olive oil. Spread the ricotta over the rounds and distribute the zucchini and sausage topping over the rounds; sprinkle with the shredded cheese.

If using a baking stone or tiles, place one pan on the stone or tiles. Otherwise, place one pan on the middle shelf of the oven. Bake the 4-inch pizzette for 5 minutes and the 6-inch pizzette for 6 or 7 minutes, or until the crusts are crisp and lightly browned on the bottom. Sprinkle with the herbs and serve immediately. Repeat to bake the remaining pizzette.

Makes twenty-four 4-inch or sixteen 6-inch pizzette

SAUSAGE and MUSHROOM PIZZETTE

The new specialty sausages offer many flavor possibilities to update America's favorite pepperoni topping. The sauce may be made in advance.

Basic, Whole-Wheat Bran, Four-Grain, or Cornmeal Pizzetta Dough

Tomato Sauce

2 tablespoons olive oil, preferably extra-virgin

2 large yellow onions, finely chopped (2 cups)

1 carrot, peeled and shredded

4 garlic cloves, minced

Two 28-ounce cans Roma (plum) tomatoes, chopped

½ cup dry red wine

Salt and freshly ground black pepper to taste

3 tablespoons minced fresh oregano or basil

Mix and knead the dough, then set it aside to rise.

Meanwhile, to make the tomato sauce: In a saucepan over medium-low heat, heat the olive oil and sauté the onions and carrot until soft, about 5 minutes. Stir in the garlic, tomatoes and their juice, and wine and boil gently, stirring occasionally, until thickened, about 20 to 25 minutes. Season with salt, pepper, and oregano or basil. Let cool.

Twenty minutes before baking, preheat the oven to 475°F. If using a baking stone or tiles, preheat the oven for 30 minutes with the stone or tiles on the bottom shelf of the oven. Cut the dough into quarters, cut each piece of dough into sixths, and roll them into 4-inch rounds on a lightly floured surface. Or, cut the dough into quarters, then cut each of these pieces into quarters and roll them into 6-inch rounds. Place on oiled pizza pans or baking sheets and brush the rounds lightly with olive oil. Spread the shredded cheese over the pizzette and dribble with the tomato sauce; top with the sausage, mushrooms, bell pepper, and onion. If using a baking stone or tiles, place one pan on the stone or tiles. Otherwise, place one pan on the middle shelf of the oven. Bake the 4-inch pizzette for 5 minutes and the 6-inch pizzette for 6 or 7 minutes or until the crusts are crisp and browned on the bottom. Sprinkle with grated cheese and oregano or basil and serve immediately. Repeat to bake the remaining pizzette.

Makes twenty-four 4-inch or sixteen 6-inch pizzette

Olive oil, preferably extra-virgin, for brushing

2 cups (8 ounces) shredded mozzarella cheese

8 ounces chicken basil or another cooked specialty sausage, thinly sliced

4 ounces mushrooms, sliced

1 small red or yellow bell pepper, seeded, deribbed, and cut into julienne strips

1 red onion, diced

⅓ cup (about 1½ ounces) freshly grated Parmesan cheese, preferably Parmigiano Reggiano

3 tablespoons minced fresh oregano or basil

MEXICAN CHICKEN, GREEN CHILI, and JACK PIZZETTE

Spicy chilies and chicken get a cool accent with creamy cheese in these Latin-style pizzette. To serve as an entrée, complete the menu with an avocado and cherry tomato salad, sangría, and fresh mango or strawberry sorbet.

4 boned and skinned chicken breast halves (about 1 pound)

2 cups spicy tomato-based barbecue sauce

Cornmeal or Basic Pizzetta Dough

1 tablespoon olive oil, plus olive oil for brushing, preferably extra-virgin

4 fresh green Anaheims or New Mexico green chilies, seeded and diced

4 green onions with tops, chopped

6 tablespoons minced fresh cilantro

2 cups (8 ounces) shredded Monterey jack cheese

In a nonaluminum bowl, combine the chicken and 1 cup of the barbecue sauce; marinate in the refrigerator for 2 hours or overnight. Let warm to room temperature before cooking. Preheat the broiler. Place the chicken breasts on a broiler rack and broil 3 inches from the heat for 5 to 6 minutes on each side, or until opaque throughout. Let the chicken cool, then cut the meat into bite-sized pieces.

Prepare the dough. At least 20 minutes before baking, preheat the oven to 475°F. If using a baking stone or tiles, preheat the oven for 30 minutes with the stone or tiles on the bottom shelf of the oven.

In a medium skillet or sauté pan over medium heat, heat the 1 tablespoon oil and sauté the chilies and onions until soft, about 5 minutes. Mix in the chicken and half of the cilantro.

Cut the dough into quarters, cut each piece of dough into sixths, and roll them into 4-inch rounds on a lightly floured surface. Or cut the dough into quarters, then cut each of these pieces into quarters and roll them into 6-inch rounds. Place on 3 oiled pizza pans or baking sheets and brush the rounds lightly with olive oil. Sprinkle each round with cheese, then dribble with the remaining barbecue sauce and some of the chicken and chili-onion mixture.

If using a baking stone or tiles, place one pan on the stone or tiles. Otherwise, place one pan on the middle shelf of the oven. Bake the 4-inch pizzette for 5 minutes and the 6-inch pizzette for 6 or 7 minutes or until the crusts are crisp and browned on the bottom. Sprinkle with the remaining cilantro and serve immediately. Repeat to bake the remaining pizzette.

Makes twenty-four 4-inch or sixteen 6-inch pizzette

Note

Smoked chicken can substitute for the chicken breasts. Omit marinating the smoked chicken in the barbecue sauce.

EGYPTIAN SPICED LAMB and DRIED FRUIT PIZZETTE

A spicy Middle Eastern meat mixture, studded with dried cranberries and apricots, tops savory pizzette in this captivating combination. Round out the menu with a tomato and cucumber salad and roasted eggplant slices. Sip a Zinfandel, Grignolino, or Petite Sirah, and finish off with peaches or nectarines splashed with a fruity wine.

Prepare the dough. At least 20 minutes before baking, preheat the oven to 475°F. If using a baking stone or tiles, preheat the oven for 30 minutes with the stone or tiles on the bottom shelf of the oven.

In a large skillet or sauté pan over medium heat, heat the 1 tablespoon oil and sauté the onion and garlic until translucent, about 5 minutes. Add the meat, cinnamon, allspice, cumin, salt, and pepper, and sauté over medium-high heat until the meat is barely browned, about 3 minutes. Drain off the excess fat. Stir in the cranberries or cherries and apricots. Let cool.

Cut the dough into quarters, cut each piece of dough into sixths, and roll them into 4-inch rounds on a lightly floured surface. Or, cut the dough into quarters, then cut each of these pieces into quarters and roll them into 6-inch rounds. Place on 3 oiled pizza pans or baking pans.

Basic, Four-Grain, or Whole-Wheat Yogurt Pizzetta Dough

1 tablespoon olive oil, plus olive oil for brushing, preferably extra-virgin

1 large red onion, chopped

2 garlic cloves, minced

1½ pounds lean ground lamb

¼ teaspoon ground cinnamon

½ teaspoon ground allspice

¾ teaspoon ground cumin

Salt and freshly ground black pepper to taste

⅓ cup dried cranberries or cherries

⅓ cup dried apricots, chopped

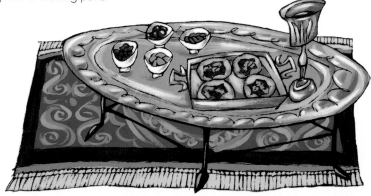

Brush the rounds lightly with oil and sprinkle with the shredded cheese. Distribute the meat filling over the rounds; sprinkle with nuts.

If using a baking stone or tiles, place one pan on the stone or tiles. Otherwise, place one pan on the middle shelf of the oven. Bake the 4-inch pizzette for 5 minutes and the 6-inch pizzette for 6 or 7 minutes, or until the crusts are crisp and lightly browned on the bottom. Top each pizzetta with grated cheese, sprinkle with parsley, and serve immediately. Repeat to bake the remaining pizzette.

Makes twenty-four 4-inch or sixteen 6-inch pizzette

2 cups (8 ounces) shredded Jarlsberg, Muenster, or jack cheese

¼ cup pine nuts or toasted sunflower seeds

1 cup (4 ounces) freshly grated Parmesan cheese, preferably Parmigiano Reggiano

3 tablespoons minced fresh flat-leaf (Italian) parsley

sweet

pizzette

ALMONDS

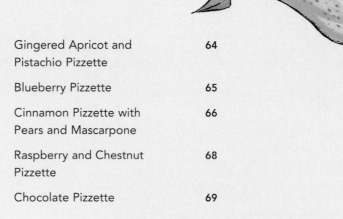

GINGERED APRICOT and PISTACHIO PIZZETTE

For a luscious treat at brunch, tea, or dessert, offer these pizzette combining tangy apricots, ginger-spiked cheese, and a crisp crust. If convenient, bake the crusts ahead of time, and freeze them if you wish, ready to top at the last minute.

Sweet or Chestnut Pizzetta Dough

1 egg white, slightly beaten

1³/₄ cups yogurt cheese (see page 49), or 12 ounces natural cream cheese, at room temperature

¹/₃ cup chopped candied ginger

12 apricots or 6 nectarines, halved, pitted, and sliced

¹/₄ cup pistachios or pine nuts

3 tablespoons raw sugar or brown sugar

Prepare the dough. At least 20 minutes before baking, preheat the oven to 475°F. If using a baking stone or tiles, preheat the oven for 30 minutes with the stone or tiles on the bottom shelf of the oven.

Divide the dough into quarters, cut each piece of dough into sixths, and roll them into 4-inch rounds on a floured surface. Or, cut the dough into quarters, then cut each of these pieces into quarters and roll them into 6-inch rounds. Place on 3 oiled pizza pans or baking sheets. Brush the dough with slightly beaten egg white and prick it with a fork.

If using a baking stone or tiles, place one pan on the stone or tiles. Otherwise, place one pan on the middle shelf of the oven. Bake for 5 minutes, or until firm. Combine the cheese and ginger and spread over the crusts. Top with the sliced apricots or nectarines and sprinkle with the nuts and sugar. Reduce the oven temperature to 425°F and bake until the crusts are crisp and browned on the bottom, about 1 to 2 minutes. Serve immediately. Repeat to bake the remaining pizzette. If desired, the untopped crusts may be baked in advance, then topped and heated.

Makes twenty-four 4-inch or sixteen 6-inch pizzette

BLUEBERRY PIZZETTE

For a breakfast or brunch treat, offer assorted fruit-topped pizzette. The tender, sweet bread base complements a varied selection of seasonal fresh fruits.

Sweet Pizzetta Dough

1 egg white, beaten slightly

8 ounces natural cream cheese or mascarpone at room temperature

3 cups fresh or frozen blueberries or sliced fresh peaches

3 tablespoons pine nuts or sliced almonds

About 3 tablespoons powdered sugar

Prepare the dough. At least 20 minutes before baking, preheat the oven to 475° F. If using a baking stone or tiles, preheat the oven for 30 minutes with the stone or tiles on the bottom shelf of the oven.

Cut the dough into quarters, cut each piece of dough into sixths, and roll them into 4-inch rounds on a lightly floured surface. Or, cut the dough into quarters, then cut each of these pieces into quarters and roll them into 6-inch rounds. Place on 3 oiled pizza pans or baking sheets. Brush the dough lightly with the egg white. Spread the cream cheese or mascarpone over the dough and top with the fruit and nuts.

If using a baking stone or tiles, place one pan on the stone or tiles. Otherwise, place one pan on the middle shelf of the oven. Bake the 4-inch pizzette for 5 minutes and the 6-inch pizzette for 6 to 7 minutes, or until the crusts are crisp and browned on the bottom. Dust with powdered sugar shaken through a sieve and serve immediately. Repeat to bake the remaining pizzette.

Makes twenty-four 4-inch or sixteen 6-inch pizzette

CINNAMON PIZZETTE with PEARS and MASCARPONE

These delectable fruit tartlets suit most any occasion of the day: breakfast, coffee hour, or dessert. Other cheeses such as Gorgonzola or a fresh mild goat cheese may replace the mascarpone or Brie.

Cinnamon-Sugar Pizzetta Dough

1 egg white, beaten slightly

6 ounces mascarpone or Brie, rind removed, and thinly sliced

6 Bartlett or Anjou pears, very thinly sliced

3 tablespoons dried cranberries

3 tablespoons sliced or slivered almonds

3 tablespoons sugar

½ teaspoon ground cinnamon

Prepare the dough. At least 20 minutes before baking, preheat the oven to 475°F. If using a baking stone or tiles, preheat the oven for 30 minutes with the stone or tiles on the bottom shelf of the oven.

Cut the dough into quarters, cut each piece of dough into sixths, and roll them into 4-inch rounds on a floured surface. Or cut the piece of dough into quarters, then cut each of these pieces into quarters and roll them into 6-inch rounds. Place on 3 oiled pizza pans and baking pans. Brush the rounds with egg white or spread with mascarpone or cover with Brie. Top with the pears, cranberries, and nuts. Mix together the sugar and cinnamon and sprinkle over.

If using a baking stone or tiles, place one pan on the stone or tiles. Otherwise, place one pan on the middle shelf of the oven. Bake the 4-inch pizzette for 5 minutes and the 6-inch pizzette for 6 to 7 minutes, or until the crusts are crisp and browned on the bottom. Serve immediately. Repeat to bake the remaining pizzette.

Makes twenty-four 4-inch or sixteen 6-inch pizzette

Apple Variation

Instead of the pears, peel, core, and thinly slice 6 Granny Smith or McIntosh apples. In a large skillet or sauté pan over medium heat, melt 2 tablespoons butter and sauté the apples with 1 tablespoon sugar, stirring, until tender, about 10 minutes. Let cool.

RASPBERRY and CHESTNUT PIZZETTE

Raspberries and creamy cheese create an ambrosial topping for sweet crusts made with starchy, low-fat chestnuts and chestnut flour.

Chestnut Pizzetta Dough

1 egg white, slightly beaten

12 ounces natural cream cheese or St. André or other triple-crème cheese at room temperature

3 tablespoons pine nuts

3 cups raspberries or halved strawberries

3 ounces white or bittersweet chocolate, shaved

Prepare the dough. At least 20 minutes before baking, preheat the oven to 475°F. If using a baking stone or tiles, preheat the oven for 30 minutes with the stone or tiles on the bottom shelf of the oven.

Cut the dough into quarters, cut each piece of dough into sixths, and roll them into 4-inch rounds. Or, cut the dough into quarters, then cut each of these pieces into quarters and roll them into 6-inch rounds. Place on 3 oiled pizza pans or baking sheets. Brush the dough with slightly beaten egg white and prick it with a fork.

If using a baking stone or tiles, place one pan on the stone or tiles. Otherwise, place one pan on the middle shelf of the oven. Bake in the oven for 4 minutes, or until firm. Spread the cheese over the rounds and sprinkle with the nuts. Continue baking until the crusts are crisp and browned on the bottom, about 1 to 2 minutes longer. Top with berries, sprinkle with shaved chocolate, and serve immediately. Repeat to bake the remaining pizzette. If desired, the crusts may be baked ahead, then topped and heated.

Makes twenty-four 4-inch or sixteen 6-inch pizzette

CHOCOLATE PIZZETTE

Serve this version of *pain au chocolat*, the chocolate-filled croissant, with espresso for an afternoon or after-dinner treat.

Orange Zest Pizzetta Dough

8 ounces bittersweet chocolate

Chopped toasted hazelnuts or pistachios

Prepare the dough. At least 20 minutes before baking, preheat the oven to 475°F. If using a baking stone or tiles, preheat the oven for 30 minutes with the stone or tiles on the bottom shelf of the oven.

Cut the dough into quarters, cut each piece of dough into sixths, and roll them into 4-inch rounds. Or, cut the dough into quarters, then cut each of these pieces into quarters and roll them into 6-inch rounds. Place on 3 oiled pizza pans or baking sheets and prick the dough with a fork.

If using a baking stone or tiles, place one pan on the stone or tiles. Otherwise, place one pan on the middle shelf of the oven. Bake the 4-inch pizzette for 5 minutes and the 6-inch pizzette for 6 to 7 minutes, or until the crusts are crisp and browned on the bottom. Meanwhile, melt the chocolate in a small bowl over hot water or in a microwave. Spread one-third of the chocolate over the pizzette and sprinkle with nuts. Serve immediately. Repeat to bake the remaining pizzette. If desired, the crusts may be baked in advance, then reheated for 1 or 2 minutes in a preheated 475°F oven and topped.

Makes twenty-four 4-inch or sixteen 6-inch pizzette

index

equivalents

Weights

US/UK	Metric
1 oz	30 g
2 oz	60 g
3 oz	90 g
4 oz (¼ lb)	125 g
5 oz (⅓ lb)	155 g
6 oz	185 g
7 oz	220 g
8 oz (½ lb)	250 g
10 oz	315 g
12 oz (¾ lb)	375 g
14 oz	440 g
16 oz (1 lb)	500 g
1½ lb	750 g
2 lb	1 kg
3 lb	1.5 kg

Liquids

US	Metric	UK
2 tbl	30 ml	1 fl oz
¼ cup	60 ml	2 fl oz
⅓ cup	80 ml	3 fl oz
½ cup	125 ml	4 fl oz
⅔ cup	160 ml	5 fl oz
¾ cup	180 ml	6 fl oz
1 cup	250 ml	8 fl oz
1½ cups	375 ml	12 fl oz
2 cups	1 l	32 fl oz

Oven Temperatures

F.	Celsius	Gas
250	120	½
275	140	1
300	150	2
325	160	3
350	180	4
375	190	5
400	200	6
425	220	7
450	230	8
475	240	9
500	260	10

Length Measures

⅛ in	3 mm
¼ in	6 mm
½ in	12 mm
1 in	2.5 cm
2 in	5 cm
3 in	7.5 cm
4 in	10 cm
5 in	13 cm
6 in	15 cm
7 in	18 cm
8 in	20 cm
9 in	23 cm
10 in	25 cm
11 in	28 cm
12 in/1 ft	30 cm

The exact equivalents in the preceding tables have been rounded for convenience.

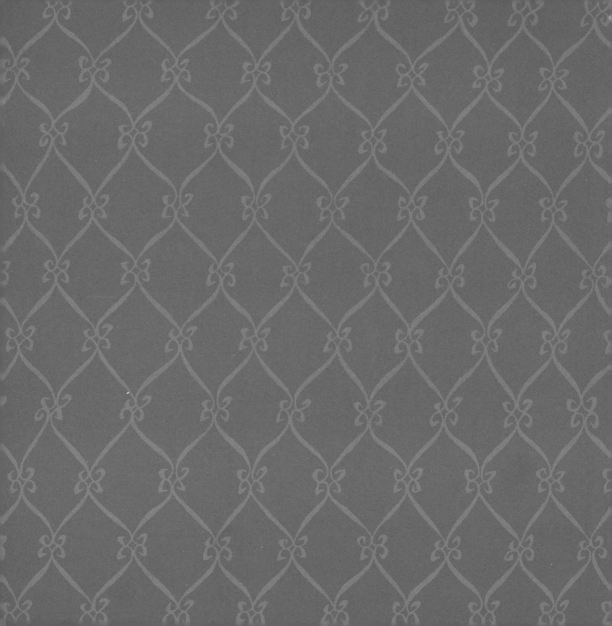